RUSKIN BOND

THE LITTLE BOOK OF COMFORT

PENGUIN
VIKING

An imprint of Penguin Random House

VIKING

USA | Canada | UK | Ireland | Australia
New Zealand | India | South Africa | China

Viking is part of the Penguin Random House group of companies
whose addresses can be found at global.penguinrandomhouse.com

Published by Penguin Random House India Pvt. Ltd
7th Floor, Infinity Tower C, DLF Cyber City,
Gurgaon 122 002, Haryana, India

First published in Viking by Penguin Random House India 2019

Copyright © Ruskin Bond 2019

ISBN 9780670092291

Illustrations by Tarun Deep Girdher
Book design by Ahlawat Gunjan and Akangksha Sarmah
Printed at Replika Press Pvt. Ltd, India

www.penguin.co.in

Introduction

Just the other evening when I was a little disheartened, I chanced across a line in one of my notebooks. 'The night is not really so dark as it seems. . .'

So I went out into the night, walked up the hill, discovered new things about the night and myself, and came home refreshed. For just as the night has the moon and the stars, so the darkness of the soul can be lit up by the small fireflies—such as these calm and comforting thoughts that I have jotted down for you. . .

AS ONE
DOOR SHUTS
ANOTHER
OPENS.

go outdoors,
it is better
to hear the bulbul sing
than the mouse squeak.

ACQUIRE
KNOWLEDGE.
ACQUIRE SKILLS.

THEY WEIGH NOTHING,
AND YOU CAN CARRY
THEM WITH YOU
ALL YOUR LIFE.

It is a good
test of memory
to try and recall
what you were
worrying about
last week.

SOMETHING
ATTEMPTED
MAY FAIL.

INACTION,

HOWEVER,
MUST FAIL.

THE MOST
CREATIVE MOMENTS
HAVE ALWAYS ARISEN
AT TIMES WHEN
CIRCUMSTANCES APPEARED
MOST HOPELESS.

WHICH IS THE
BEST GAME ?

THERE ISN'T ONE.

IF THE PLAYER
IS DOING THE BEST,
HIS GAME IS
THE FINEST.

A depression
is a period
when
people are
obliged to do
without things
their forefathers
never had.

Be as interested
as you possibly can
in all things —
and especially
interested in
some things.

The sweetest and wisest
people have probably
experienced bad luck.

This is what
has made them
sweet and wise.

for any beauty
you possess
at sixteen,
be very grateful.

Of the beauty you have
at sixty, you may be proud —
it is your own
achievement.

THINGS WILL
DON'T
OFTEN COME
COMPLAIN
RIGHT BY
TOO MUCH
THEMSELVES.

STUDY THE FACE
OF NATURE
   AND YOU WILL
NEVER BE
   BORED.

DO NOT PRAY
FOR AN
EASY LIFE.
PRAY INSTEAD
TO BE A
**STRONGER
PERSON.**

BEFORE
YOU GET UPSET,
ASK YOURSELF:

*does it
really matter?*

BELIEVE
IN YOURSELF.
SOON
OTHERS WILL
BELIEVE
IN you too.

Help a stranger
in distress,
and one day
you may receive
help when you
least expect it.

MOST IDEAS
NEVER WORK —

UNLESS
YOU MAKE SURE
THEY DO.

VALUE GOOD FRIENDS.
REMEMBER
COLERIDGE'S WORDS,
"*Friendship
is a sheltering
tree.*"

It is good that others succeed.

Do not allow their successes to cast a shadow on your efforts.

CONSIDER YOURSELF DEAD,
AND THAT YOU HAVE
COMPLETED YOUR LIFE
UPTO THE PRESENT TIME,
THEN
START LIVING
AS THOUGH YOUR LIFE
HAS BEEN GIFTED
TO YOU AGAIN.

Don't be depressed
by your surroundings –

that pebble at your foot
has as much beauty
as any
great work of art.

YOUR ROOM

MUST
    LOOK AT THE CLOUDS
HAVE A
    LOOK AT THE STARS
WINDOW—
    LOOK AT THE GOOD
    BROWN EARTH.

THERE IS MONEY
TO BE MADE
IN THE MARKETPLACE,
BUT UNDER
A SHADY TREE
there is rest.

STEP OUT
LIGHTLY,
STEP OUT
BRIGHTLY,
AND LUCK WILL
COME YOUR
WAY.

AVOID
QUARRELS.
YOU WILL FIND THAT
MOST QUARRELS
ARE WEAK
ON BOTH SIDES.

sow an act,
reap a habit.
sow a habit,
reap a character.
sow a character,
reap a destiny.

THE WISEST MAN

IS HE WHO

DOESN'T THINK

HE IS.

TO FIND
HAPPINESS,
LOOK HALFWAY
BETWEEN TOO LITTLE
AND TOO MUCH.

DON'T GIVE UP.

ONE SUCCESS
WILL ERASE
MANY FAILURES.

Never measure
   your generosity
   by what you give,
but rather by
what you have left.

IF WE FEAR SOMEONE,
WE GIVE THAT PERSON
POWER OVER US.
SO BE GENTLE,
BUT DON'T ALLOW
YOURSELF TO
BE TROD UPON.

DON'T LET
PETTY-MINDED PEOPLE
PREVENT YOU FROM
DOING YOUR THING.

dogs may bark

BUT THE CARAVAN
MOVES ON.

SOME OF US ARE
LIKE TEA LEAVES.
WE DON'T KNOW
OUR REAL STRENGTH
UNTIL WE ARE
IN HOT WATER.

Avoid people who
make long speeches.

The less a man knows
the longer he takes
to tell it.

THERE ARE NO FRESH
STARTS IN LIFE.

BUT THERE ARE
NEW DIRECTIONS.

LEARN TO ZIG-ZAG.

By all means
observe the conventions,
but remember
that it is only in
personal independence
that happiness
is to be found.
Stay free!

BE TRANQUIL
DO NOT PLAN LIFE
TOO EAGERLY.

FOLLOW YOUR INTUITIONS;
TAKE GRATEFULLY
THE JOYS OF LIFE; AND
        LEAVE THE REST TO GOD.

TRY LOVING

YOUR ENEMIES.

IF NOTHING ELSE,

YOU'LL CONFUSE THEM.

TAKE A CHANCE
THE TURTLE
ONLY MAKES PROGRESS
WHEN IT STICKS
ITS NECK OUT.

Let no man take
your dreams away.
They will sustain you
to the end.

DO WHAT

YOU KNOW BEST,

AND DO IT WELL.

ACT IMPECCABLY,

EVERYTHING WILL THEN

FALL INTO PLACE.

THE GREATEST

VICTORY IS

THE ONE YOU

win over

yourself.

If you are the target
   of other people's envy
remember, it is only
   at trees that
   bear good fruit
      that
slones are thrown.

IF YOU LIVE
FOR YOURSELF ALONE,
YOU ARE IN
GREAT DANGER OF
BEING BORED
TO DEATH.

LIFE IS NOT

SOMETHING

TO PUT UP WITH,

BUT A

gift to be

enjoyed

WITH ZEST.

COURTESY IS

A POWERFUL WEAPON —

THE MORE SO WHEN

USED IN THE FACE OF

ARROGANCE AND HOSTILITY.

Grandfather said,

'If you cannot win,

make the fellow

ahead of you exert

himself to the utmost!'

HE
WHO IS ALWAYS TRYING, IS DOING; AND HE WHO IS ALWAYS DOING, **DOES.**

Life
will always give
US WHAT

WE KNOW WE ARE WORTH.

It never fails

TO TAKE US AT OUR

OWN VALUATION.

EVERY DAY,

NOT CHRISTMAS,

AND EVERY DAY

NOT RAINY DAY.

~WEST INDIAN PROVERB.

Almost anyone
can do the first
half of anything;

only those who do
the second half
arrive.

ADVERSITY IS ALWAYS
INTERMITTENT;
THEREFORE,
IF EFFORT IS
CONSTANT,
*you are bound
to win.*

'How shall we
hoodwink them?'

ASKED THE YOUNG DEMON
OF THE OLD STORY.

'Tell them there's
plenty of time'

SAID THE OLD DEMON
OF EXPERIENCE.

'Lots of time.
they always
fall for that.'

go and
DO THINGS
you are bound
to succeed
in some of them.

THANK GOD

FOR BEGINNINGS.
NEW YEARS, NEW MONTHS,
NEW WEEKS—
AFTER EVERY TWENTY-FOUR HOURS
A NEW DAY,
WITH THE SUN
RISING OVER A NEW WORLD.

You will sometimes
be punished when
you do not deserve it.

Before giving vent to
your indignation,
reflect on how often
you have
deserved punishment
without receiving it.

IF YOU CAN

SMILE

WHEN YOU FEEL HURT,

THE HURT IS HALF CURED.

IF YOU VISIT YOUR
    BEAN AND LETTUCE
MERCHANT EVERY DAY,
YOU WON'T HAVE
    TO VISIT YOUR CHEMIST.

IF YOU HAVE MUCH,
GIVE OF YOUR WEALTH.
IF YOU HAVE LITTLE,
GIVE OF YOUR HEART.

MAKE SURE

ALL YOUR TAXES

HAVE BEEN PAID,

AND THEN

SIT DOWN AND

enjoy a
        good meal.

IF YOU
WANT TO
TRAVEL FAST,
KEEP TO THE
OLD ROADS.

Be guarded
in your speech.

Don't talk too much.
many words
initiate
many defeats.

WINNERS
HANG ON
WHEN LOSERS
LET GO,

THE STRONG
MAN AND
THE WATERFALL
CHANNEL
THEIR OWN
PATHS.

If you have
good health,
you are young;
and
if you owe
nothing
you are rich.

ONE
COURAGEOUS
THOUGHT
WILL PUT TO
FLIGHT A HOST
OF TROUBLES.

NOBODY GROWS OLD
MERELY BY LIVING
A CERTAIN NUMBER
OF YEARS.

FAILURE
IS NOT ~~DEFEAT~~.
IT IS JUST
LEARNING HOW.

The sage lives
         in yesterday;
the dreamer
         in tomorrow;
the plodder in today.

The successful man
   combines all three.

THEY ALWAYS

COME SO QUICKLY —

THOSE TURNING POINTS

IN LIFE —

AND ALWAYS

DOWN A LANE WE

ARE NOT WATCHING

There is always
suitable work
for every season.

That is why we
need not fear old age.

PROGRESS
SOMETIMES
USES A COMMA,

BUT NEVER
A FULL STOP.

YOU CAN
GENERALLY
GET SUCCESS
IF YOU DO
NOT WANT
VICTORY.

The difficult
can be done
immediately;

the impossible
takes a little longer.

It's of no great
consequence
    in this world
    who lets you down,
    so long as
it isn't yourself.

A LOST BATTLE

IS A BATTLE

~~one believes~~

LOST.

'WELL BEGUN
IS HALF DONE'

YES, BUT REMEMBER

'HALF DONE'
IS ONLY
HALF DONE.

stay still within,
    even if the world
around you is
all sound and fury.

Be like water.
There's no stopping it.
No matter how tiny
the trickle,
it will eventually
get somewhere.

NOW AND THEN
THERE COMES A TIME
IN OUR AFFAIRS
WHEN
COURAGE IS SAFER
THAN PRUDENCE.

YOU WILL FIND
LIFE EXACTLY
AS YOU TAKE IT,
MAKE IT, LIVE IT,
AND GIVE IT.

The great successes
of the world
have been the
results of a second,
a third,
even a
fiftieth attempt.

BE USEFUL,
BE WANTED,
BE NECESSARY.

THERE IS NO
LIFE FOR
THOSE WHO
AREN'T.

How many dreams
    might have become
happy realities
    but for that
    terrible little sentence,
'too much trouble!'

WHEN

IT PAYS BETTER

TO TALK

THAN TO LISTEN,

change

YOUR

COMPANY.

To succeed in anything
you have to care
desperately for the
thing itself
and not for what
it brings with it.

WHAT HAVE
WE TO EXPECT?

ANYTHING

WHAT HAVE
WE TO FEAR?

NOTHING

WHAT HAVE WE
TO HOPE FOR?

EVERYTHING

Most men want
their children to
be a credit
to them.
Wise men try
to be a credit
to their children.

When a difficulty
presents itself,
remove it at once
if you can,
for the longer
you look at it
the less you will
like it.

HAVE
THE WISDOM
TO BE
SIMPLE,
AND THE
HUMOUR
TO BE
HAPPY!

When we go
for berries
we must not
retreat
from briars.

IF AT TIMES
LIFE SEEMS
A BATTLE,

said grandfather,

WELL THEN,
ENJOY
THE BATTLE.

'God gave us
our faces',

SAID GRANNY.

'We give ourselves
our expressions.'

Bad times are good times to prepare for better times.

*'live and
let live'*

IS A GOOD
MAXIM BUT,

*'live and
help live'*

IS A
BETTER
ONE.

WHAT IF
YOU FAILED
YESTERDAY?

TODAY
IS NOT
YESTERDAY,
IS IT?

THE MOMENT
WE CAN VISUALIZE
POSSIBILITIES,

THE ACTUALITIES
ARE NOT
VERY FAR AWAY.

If you are
capable of
smiling,

no one will bother
whether you are
good looking
or not.

The reason why
few people succeed
in moving mountains
is that few of them
practise on molehills.

BE HONEST,
Give your OPINION
FOR WHAT
IT IS WORTH;
THAT IS,
IF YOU ARE
ASKED FOR IT!

There is no
dependence
that can be certain
but a dependence
on yourself.

THE ONLY
EDUCATED
PERSON
IS THE
SELF
EDUCATED.

IT IS ONLY

THROUGH HUMILITY

THAT WE ARE

ABLE TO PRESERVE

OUR DIGNITY.

What you think
    of yourself
is more important
    than what others
    think of you.

To LIVE
IN PEACE
WITH OTHERS

FIRST
MAKE PEACE
WITH
YOURSELF.

Chart your own
course through life.

What the stars
foretell is strictly
for astrologers.

Before you discuss
anyone's faults,
    take time
    to count to ten...

ten of your own.

A SOFT
ANSWER
TURNS
AWAY
ANGER.

If you can rule
your own spirit,
you are stronger
than the man
who rules a city.

A PICTURE
ON THE WALL

IS NOT JUST
SOMETHING
TO LOOK AT.

AFTER A TIME
IT BECOMES
COMPANY.

BETTER
A FRIEND
WHO IS NEAR
THAN A
BROTHER
WHO IS
FAR AWAY.

A merry heart
does
more good
than any medicine.

WHOEVER
SCORNS
THE POOR
REVILES
HIS OWN
MAKER.

DESTINY IS
SIMPLY THE
STRENGTH
OF YOUR
DESIRES.

written
somewhere,

'WE DIE ONLY WHEN THE WILL DIES.'

If you can't see
the bottom
of the pond,
don't try
wading in it.

THE RIGHT SORT OF
SMILE WILL CARRY YOU
ANYWHERE AND WIN
you ANYTHING.
IT MAKES PEOPLE FORGET
THAT THEY HAVE A
GRUDGE AGAINST you.

People who have
only one idea become
   terrible bores.
An idea may be good
but it is never
good enough to
claim your entire
waking life.

We are happy
in the pursuit
of success.

But having got there,
we find that
all the fun was
in climbing.

HE IS INDEED SUCCESSFUL
WHO CAUSES THE HUMAN SOUL
TO GROW ALRIGHT.

AND HE IS INDEED A
A FAILURE
WHO STUNTS AND STARVES IT.

– the Koran

Honour your food;
receive it thankfully;

eat it contentedly and joyfully,
never hold it in contempt.

Avoid excess,
for gluttony is hateful
and leads to death.

— Manu

NOTHING BODILY ACCOUNTS
FOR PERSONALITY.

AT THE BACK OF EVERYTHING,
PHYSICAL, AND GREATER
THAN ANYTHING PHYSICAL IS

the mind.

IT IS ONLY
IN HIS HEAD
THAT MAN
IS HEROIC.

IN THE PIT
OF HIS STOMACH
HE IS ALWAYS
A COWARD.

There is comfort—
to be had
from an old book.

The fact that it
has been around
for so long,
with its thoughts,
feelings and words,
gives one a feeling
of permanence.

A good man
can never die.
The person of a man
may be taken away,
but the best part
of a good man
lives on.

AS WE GROW
OLDER,
WE BECOME
BRAVER.
WE ARE NO
LONGER
AFRAID OF
THE DARK.

Do your best.

IN THAT WAY

SERVE THE BEAUTIFUL.

YOU ACHIEVE

FOLLOW THE TRUTH.

SELF - RESPECT.

Grandfather's advice was
to have five years'
income in hand
before starting
to build a house.

A WISE MAN SAID:

Do not condemn
the judgement of
another because
it differs from
your own. You may
both be wrong.

SMILES
ARE BORN,
NOT MADE.
IF THEY
ARE FORCED,
THEY ARE NOT
SMILES BUT
GRIMACES.

REACH FOR
THE SKY.

EVEN IF
YOU CAN'T
TOUCH IT.
you will be
an arm's
length nearer.

Some people are
always complaining
    because
roses have thorns.
Let us be grateful that
    thorns have roses

as Gertrude Stein
once said,

'money is
      always there
but the pocket
      changes.'

TIME IS

TOO SLOW FOR

THOSE WHO WAIT

TOO SWIFT FOR

THOSE WHO FEAR

TOO LONG FOR

THOSE WHO GRIEVE

TOO SHORT FOR

THOSE WHO REJOICE

BUT FOR THOSE

WHO LOVE

TIME IS ETERNITY.

—INSCRIBED ON

ON A SUNDIAL

About The Author

Ruskin Bond, one of India's best-loved writers, has written over 500 short stories, essays and novellas, and more than forty books for children. He received the Sahitya Akademi Award in 1992, the Padma Shri in 1999 and the Padma Bhushan in 2014.